Welco

NAOMI STARKEY

Describing somebody as a 'fiery' person is not usually a compliment. By choosing the word 'fiery' we tend to mean 'fierce, intolerant, hot-tempered'. At the same time, to say that we are 'fired up' by something means that we are enthusiastic, ready to throw ourselves into a situation or activity with boundless energy and vigour.

While we may talk about faith being 'kindled', what does it actually mean to be 'on fire' for God? Traditional 'hellfire and brimstone' preachers don't tend to get a good press these days, and then there is always the danger of 'burnout' when things just get too hot for us...

In this issue of *Quiet Spaces*, we focus on different aspects of fire, both positive and negative. This powerful symbol appears many times in the Bible, particularly as an image for God himself, from the guiding pillar of fire at the time of the exodus to the tongues of flame on the day of Pentecost. In other contexts, we reflect on how 'guarding the flame' can have positive overtones of nurture and maintaining a witness. Taking yet another angle, while a fierce fire may leave a heap of ashes, God promises to bring beauty and healing even out of such remains.

Before the age of electricity, any kind of light involved actual fire and heat, whether a gas mantle, candles or (remembering the old chorus 'Sing hosanna') the biblical oil lamp that needed topping up with fuel in order to stay 'burning till the break of day'. To adapt a well-known saying, it is worth remembering that even a very small candle flame can bring both warmth and light to cold, dark places.

Naomi Starkey

1

This compilation copyright © BRF 2007
Illustrations copyright © Chris Daunt, Ian Mitchell, Ray and Corinne Burrows 2007
Authors retain copyright in their own work

Published by
The Bible Reading Fellowship
15 The Chambers, Vineyard
Abingdon OX14 3FE
Websites: www.brf.org.uk and www.quietspaces.org.uk

ISBN 978 1 84101 500 2
First published 2007
10 9 8 7 6 5 4 3 2 1 0
All rights reserved

Acknowledgments
Scripture quotations taken from The New Revised Standard Version of the Bible, Anglicized Edition, copyright © 1989, 1995 by the Division of Christian Education of the National Council of the Churches of Christ in the USA, are used by permission. All rights reserved.

Scripture quotations taken from the Holy Bible, New International Version, copyright © 1973, 1978, 1984 by International Bible Society, are used by permission of Hodder & Stoughton Publishers, a division of Hodder Headline Ltd. All rights reserved. 'NIV' is a registered trademark of International Bible Society. UK trademark number 1448790.

Scripture quotations taken from The Revised Standard Version of the Bible, copyright © 1946, 1952, 1971 by the Division of Christian Education of the National Council of the Churches of Christ in the USA, are used by permission. All rights reserved.

Scripture quotations taken from the Holy Bible, Today's New International Version. Copyright © 2004 by International Bible Society. Used by permission of Hodder & Stoughton Publishers, a division of Hodder Headline Ltd. All rights reserved. 'TNIV' is a registered trademark of International Bible Society.

Scriptures from the New English Bible copyright © 1961, 1970 by Oxford University Press and Cambridge University Press.

Extracts from The Book of Common Prayer of 1662, the rights of which are vested in the Crown in perpetuity within the United Kingdom, are reproduced by permission of Cambridge University Press, Her Majesty's Printers.

'The Beloved' by Eunice M. Cater, from Even Angels Tread Softly, a Mothers' Union anthology of poetry (ISBN 978 0 85943 064 7), used by permission. The Mothers' Union, 24 Tufton Street, London SW1P 3RB. Tel: 0207 222 5533. Website: www.themothersunion.org

A catalogue record for this book is available from the British Library

Printed by Gutenberg Press, Tarxien, Malta

Quiet Spaces

CONTENTS

Fire
on the mountain

Andrew Watson and his wife Bev live in south-west London, where Andrew has been the vicar of St Stephen's, East Twickenham, for the past ten years. His book 'The Fourfold Leadership of Jesus' is due to be published by BRF in 2008.

The world is charged with the grandeur of God.
It will flame out, like shining from shook foil;
It gathers to a greatness, like the ooze of oil
Crushed.

Fire is a powerful image in Gerard Manley Hopkins' famous poem 'God's grandeur' and in the biblical narratives that inspired it. The sweet-smelling sacrifice, the burning bush, the purifying fire, the flames of hell: all play a key role in the biblical understanding of God, of humanity, of sacrifice, of judgment. Fire can warm and comfort when kept within the confines of, say, an elegant Victorian fireplace, but the biblical images tend to move beyond such cosy domesticity and into a world that is wilder, more unpredictable: a dazzling world, and at some points a dangerous one.

Elijah might be described as the original fiery prophet. The twin themes of fire and mountains dominate his story, which occupies a central place in the books of Kings (1 Kings 17 through to 2 Kings 2). Early on in the narrative, a widow is gathering sticks to cook a last supper for herself and her son, and is amazed at the Lord's provision as she steps out in faith and offers hospitality to the prophet. A few chapters later, it is Elisha who is lighting a fire—this time to burn his ploughing equipment and to cook his oxen, the symbol of a decision to break with the past and embrace a new calling as Elijah's attendant.

In 2 Kings 1, the fire of judgment falls on two companies of soldiers sent by King Ahaziah to arrest Elijah (a terrible reminder of how innocent people get caught up in the machinations of their rulers), while the following chapter famously describes the 'chariot of fire' (2:11) in which Elijah is taken up to heaven— an image whose power is still celebrated in a stadium near where I live, where 70,000 rugby fans regularly bellow out the old spiritual, 'Swing low, sweet chariot'.

The most famous fire in the Elijah story, though, appears on Mount Carmel in 1 Kings 18, that great contest between Elijah and the prophets of Baal and Asherah, where a single act of divine power—fire falling on Elijah's sacrifice—brings both judgment and spiritual renewal in equal measure. At the climax of that chapter, all of God's people fall prostrate on their faces and proclaim, 'Jehovah is God! Jehovah is God!' Since the name Elijah means literally 'Jehovah is God', here is the glorious highpoint in the ministry of a prophet whose name and mission statement are one and the same.

'Fire on the mountain'—there are many other examples in scripture. We think of the fire on Mount Sinai,

A world that is wilder, more unpredictable: a dazzling world, and at some points a dangerous one

Judgment and spiritual renewal in equal measure

which, like the burning bush of a previous encounter with the Almighty, speaks of the holiness and majesty of God and left its mark on the radiant face of Moses, his prophet (Exodus 34:29). There was fire on the temple mount when Solomon and the priests were dazzled by the glory of the Lord as their sacrifices were consumed at the temple's dedication (2 Chronicles 7:1–3). We think of the fire on the mount of transfiguration, where Jesus' clothes 'became as bright as a flash of lightning' (Luke 9:29), and the disciples saw him in his glory with Moses on one side, Elijah on the other. Then there are the visions of Isaiah the prophet and John the seer—

visions of one high and lifted up, with fire purifying the lips and fire bringing judgment (Isaiah 6:1–7; Revelation 8:5).

But it's Mount Zion and the day of Pentecost that introduce us to, arguably, the most significant fire of them all: the 'tongues of flame' that came to rest on the disciples as they worshipped together in Jerusalem (Acts 2:1–3). There weren't any deaths on that occasion, unlike the day of Elijah's dramatic confrontation with the prophets of Baal, but the decision that faced God's people was every bit as serious. Would they accept Jesus as their Messiah or would they side with those whose cold legalism had led to his crucifixion?

The fire of the Spirit brought renewed holiness, love, power, passion, courage and conviction on that day. It also led a large crowd of

Fire purifying the lips and fire bringing judgment

people—three thousand in all—to respond to the call of Peter in the same spirit with which their predecessors had proclaimed, 'Jehovah is God!' And while the Jerusalem church was far from perfect, the early chapters of Acts give us some wonderful vignettes of church at its best, a church purified and

renewed by the presence of a holy God: 'Everyone was filled with awe... All the believers were together and had everything in common. Selling their possessions... they gave to anyone as he had need...' (2:42–47, NIV). It's no wonder that the early church proved so uniquely attractive to the society of its day.

How, though, are these images of fire on the mountain relevant to a generation that has largely lost touch with a world 'charged with the grandeur of God'? I believe the answer can be found in an unusual place: William Golding's novel, *The Lord of the Flies*, whose second chapter is entitled 'Fire on the mountain' and whose storyline contains many similarities to the Elijah narrative.

At the beginning of the novel, a number of boys find themselves on a desert island following a plane crash. The island is beautiful: there are fruit trees everywhere, there's sand, there are shells and, best of all, there are no grown-ups. Only the boys have survived and—to the more confident of them, at least—it's paradise.

One boy, Ralph, establishes himself as their leader, and he quickly sets a single priority for them all: to keep a fire burning on the mountain in the hope that a passing ship might see it and come to the rescue. But gradually a rival, Jack, emerges from among the boys. He and Ralph have an uneasy relationship but are held together by their fear of the beast, a grotesque flapping object that someone has

© Louise Blackmore

witnessed in the jungle. Jack's gang manages to catch and kill a pig, and they put its head on a stick as a kind of lucky charm. Before long, the pig's head is covered with insects, so that it becomes known as 'The Lord of the Flies'.

Increasingly, Ralph struggles to keep the fire alight while Jack's tribe becomes more and more violent. They cover themselves with blood and war paint, and begin openly to challenge Ralph's authority.

One of Ralph's friends, a young boy called Simon, goes away into the jungle and discovers what the beast really is—a dead parachutist hanging from a tree. He runs through the forest to report his discovery and finds Jack and his boys engaged in a pagan war dance. Whipped up into a frenzy, they kill Simon with their spears, and now that they have their first taste of human blood, it isn't long before they deliberately kill another of Ralph's friends, then go after Ralph himself.

To flush him out, they set the jungle alight, and Ralph is forced to run for his life. Ironically, the fire alerts a passing naval boat, which comes to investigate. Jack's crowd is about to kill Ralph when they are stopped in their tracks by a smartly dressed naval officer. In the face of this representative of the adult world, the boys suddenly look very small—a group of naked, dishevelled kids who have turned their paradise into the fires of hell.

Naked, dishevelled kids who have turned their paradise into the fires of hell

The parallels between the novel and the Elijah story go far beyond the theme of 'fire on the mountain', for the events on Mount Carmel remind us of two religions, two lifestyles, two rival tribes who were competing for power in the Israel of Elijah's day. Israel, the promised land, the land 'flowing with milk and honey' (Exodus 3:8), should have been a paradise where God and his people walked together in the cool of the day. But a weak king (Ahab) and a scheming queen (Jezebel) had conspired to introduce a new faith to the people of Israel—the worship of Baal—and the combination of clever marketing and the ruthless persecution of Baal's detractors meant that he, not Jehovah, was winning the ratings war.

'Baal' means 'Lord', and a fuller title in the Elijah story—'Baal Zebub'—means 'Lord of the flies' (2 Kings 1:3). The name probably originated from a belief that Baal could ward off plague and sickness—hence the accusation that Jesus was healing people and casting out demons by the power of Beelzebub (Matthew 12:24). But the reality of Baal worship was far more sinister than its origins might suggest. The mixture of pagan devotion, ritual prostitution and outright violence became so legendary that, a thousand years later, Beelzebub was still referred to as the 'Prince of demons'.

As Elijah sought to keep the light of Israel burning, as injustice and the murder of the true prophets became a daily reality, so the fire on the mountain was as potent a symbol of Elijah's leadership as that of young Ralph. Even creation itself seemed caught up in the conflict, with both the drought in Elijah's day and the conflagration in *The Lord of the Flies* giving us a timely warning of what happens when man the destroyer usurps authority from God the Creator.

Is there a God-like figure in *The Lord of the Flies*? Is he the naval officer, before whom the bullies—the Ahabs and Jezebels of this world—will stand like dishevelled children? Is he the 'beast', the half-glimpsed nightmare? Is he even Baal Zebub, the hideous pig-on-a-stick? That was, after all, the accusation made by Jesus' detractors.

The answer in the novel may be a little ambivalent, although the naval officer has more than a hint of the *deus ex machina* about him, coming to sort out the mess and take the children home; but in Elijah's story, God is the one who answers by fire—the holy God, the powerful God, the living God. Baal and his minions may look very threatening; Jezebel may even turn those threats into action; but the reality is that Baal is simply an idol, powerless to save. His prophets can dance around in their war paint for all they're worth; but only the calm authority of the prophet of the living God can bring fire—the fire of renewal, the fire of judgment.

The confrontation at Mount Carmel has an unusual postscript. Elijah's elation was shortlived as he fled for his life, exhausted and terrified (1 Kings 19:3). Strengthened by food, drink and a good night's sleep, he made his way to Mount Horeb (another name for Mount Sinai), where he expected to meet with God just as Moses had done. Initially it all looked very promising. There was a great wind, an earthquake and a fire.

Elijah had experienced such dramas on Mount Carmel and expected to do so again. Yet, we're told, 'the Lord was not in the wind... not in the earthquake... not in the fire' (vv. 11–12). And 'after the fire', we read, 'came a gentle whisper' (v.12)—or, more literally, 'after the fire came the sound of silence'.

It must have been something of an anticlimax for a prophet who'd travelled all the way to Mount Sinai, the holy mountain, the mountain of fire, yet the truth is that Elijah didn't need anything dramatic at that point. He'd had enough drama to last him a

The fire of the Spirit
brought renewed holiness, love, power, passion, courage and conviction

lifetime. What he needed was intimacy, drawing so close to God that he could pick up on the gentlest whisper, the sound of silence.

There may be a time for the fire of Pentecost, jolting us out of our complacency and filling us with the power and passion of our Lord. But there are other times, too, when we gather around the risen Christ in the intimacy of the upper room; when he simply breathes on us and speaks the words of life: 'Receive the Holy Spirit' (John 20:22). ∎

Praying and
Personality

David Runcorn is presently Director of Ministry Development in Lichfield Diocese, which involves providing training and support for men and women in all aspects of Christian ministry. He is the author of a number of books, most recently 'Spirituality Workbook' (SPCK, 2005) and 'Rumours of Life' (SPCK, 2006). He lives in Derby in his wife's vicarage with their two sons.

God loves variety.
In all he creates, he never repeats himself

In the few glimpses we have into the life of heaven, we find a community of strikingly different creatures joyfully united around the throne of God in timeless worship: 'Holy, holy, holy, the Lord God the Almighty, who was and is and is to come' (Revelation 4:6–8, NRSV). Any worship leader who has struggled to cater for the contradictory tastes of earthly congregations would love to know the secret!

God loves variety. In all he creates, he never repeats himself. The nearer we get to him, the *more* different we become from each other, not less. 'Everything in heaven comes apart,' writes the poet Stewart Henderson. By that he means that in heaven each created thing will be fully revealed in its uniqueness and distinctiveness, celebrating its place in the whole that is the glorious life of God. When we pray '... on earth as it is in heaven', we are asking, among other things, for the same bewildering mixture to be a feature of our lives, too.

This also means that the number of ways of praying will be as varied and different as there are people. There is no right way to pray. God never comes to us with an 'off-the-peg' method of praying that we have to use regardless of our personality, gifts or needs.

I always need reminding of this

© Tom Grill/Corbis

11

God lovingly works 'with the grain' of the person he has made us to be

There is no right way to pray

because, at a formative stage in my Christian life, the message that I heard was quite the opposite. Certain ways of believing and praying were the 'correct' ones. Other ways were looked on with suspicion. Furthermore, I was told, my own personality, thoughts and desires were obstacles to real prayer: they had to be firmly denied and pushed out of the way. Following Jesus meant having a very negative view of myself. There was also a deep suspicion of life beyond the boundaries of what was carefully (not to say rigidly) defined as Christian.

I now think that such attitudes are unbiblical and deeply damaging to our ability to sense God's presence in our lives. For all their realism about human sin, the Psalms, for example, never lose confidence that all created life is touched and renewed moment by

moment by the presence of God. Over time, I have grown to treasure the way God lovingly works 'with the grain' of the person he has made us to be—no matter how much restoring, healing and time it takes. I come as I am and he receives me with love and joy.

One of my most exciting discoveries in recent years has been the significance of our personalities in the way we relate to God. One of the best books on this is *Finding Your Prayer Personality* by Ruth Fowke (Abingdon Press, 2002). The author understands from hard experience what it is like to try to pray in someone else's style. It's like being required to wear an outfit that someone has lent us, for want of anything else on offer. It doesn't fit us; it doesn't suit us; it actually belongs to someone else. But we were told that this is how to pray so we feel condemned when we find it an uncomfortable struggle.

Ruth writes, 'God created us different from each other. He does not want our communication with him to be constricted or thwarted by stilted, imposed patterns of prayer.' She explores the ways in which different personalities meet the world and seek God. As I read, I was reminded of different people I know who experienced a breakthrough in their prayer lives as they made new discoveries about their personalities.

Sheila went on a Quiet Day for the first time and discovered that this was the way of silent prayer for which she had longed restlessly over many years. But it was not the way she had been taught, and her lively church fellowship found it hard to understand her gift.

Brian was a rather serious man with a marked preference for formal worship. He reluctantly attended a charismatic service and (after resisting the urge to walk out) was overcome by a new vision of the joy and love of God. He came to see how this part of his own personality had never been allowed to develop in a family ruled by his severe, emotionally repressed father.

John's approach to prayer took a new direction when he found himself sitting in a church service next to a group of hearing-impaired Christians, who were signing the songs and prayers. On impulse, he joined in and was suddenly aware of how much more alive he felt as he worshipped with his body rather than words. He not only felt nearer to God, he felt nearer to the world around him and to himself.

Karen was very ill in hospital. Praying felt impossible, and she was very anxious. Her daughter placed an icon of Christ by her bedside. She was deeply comforted and, with a naturalness that made her wish she had found this long before, she fixed her attention on his face and prayed silently using her eyes alone. Karen had always delighted in life through the 'here and now' senses—touch, smell, taste, sound and sight. Now she discovered that this was her most natural way to commune with God.

There is a wise saying: 'Pray as you can, not as you cannot!' (Dom John Chapman). We could go further: 'Pray as the person you are, not as the person you are not.' One of the most common causes of guilt for Christians is when we compare ourselves with someone else. Remember: God only asks us to be ourselves, no one else. But who am 'I'? What do we mean by 'my personality? And isn't this approach rather self-absorbed?

By 'my personality', we mean that unique mixture of thinking, desiring, feeling and relating that makes me 'me' and not somebody else. It gives me my distinctive shape and presence in the world. My personality is something that has been deeply influenced by factors such as biological and psychological

---

...never lose confidence that all created life is **touched and renewed moment by moment by the presence of God**

---

inheritance, experiences of home and family, health, education, work, relationships, and social and natural environment.

So who I am is firstly part of a much

wider story that involves, ultimately, the whole world around me. To be a 'person' is to be living and growing in this amazing, intricate web of influences and relationships. There is

> ...we need those around us who complement us

We are seeking shapes of prayer within which we can grow

no 'private' or 'spiritual' me, separate from the rest of life; everything connects. Christian spirituality is rooted in the adventure of living out the mystery of who I am, in the midst of the rest of life.

But the question of who we are goes deeper still. Ultimately our true identity is found in God, in whose image we are made. In fact, he is the only one who truly knows us. He sees who we are and what we may become: 'What we will be has not yet been revealed' (1 John 3:2). Christian discipleship means trusting to Jesus the mystery of who we are becoming. Our true life is known only in him. So, like the psalmist, we pray, 'Search me, O God, and know my heart… and lead me in the way everlasting' (Psalm 139:23–24).

A word of caution: we live in a chronically restless culture, constantly picking up and then discarding things when the next source of stimulation comes along. This can easily happen in prayer, too. Creative dance, icons, approaches to meditation and personality type indicators are just a few of the insights we can draw on, but they need to be used wisely. We are seeking shapes of prayer within which we can grow and allow our lives to unfold in God's grace. The process needs time, and excitement is no measure of depth.

We need to be honest if we tend to 'pick 'n' mix' in our spiritual lives, seeking new experiences of God and prayer and never staying long in any one place, uprooting whatever we have just planted. It is important to face this restlessness for what it is: we must confess our emptiness. It may be helpful to find a wise friend or spiritual guide with whom we can talk this through.

Finally, through even the most personal searching of faith, we need Christian fellowship with others— friendship, hearing and sharing God's word, breaking bread and drawing on community wisdom and support. Precisely because we may be drawn to certain ways of praying and expressing faith, we need those around us who complement us and who, by their words and the sheer fact that they are not like us, remind us of our part in the greater whole. So we journey together in prayer—an adventure into the heart of a God who never repeats himself. ∎

God in top gear

the reality of revival

Tom Smail (author of 'Praying with Paul' for BRF) spent nearly 20 years in parish ministry before joining the Fountain Trust, promoting charismatic renewal. He was Vice-Principal and Lecturer in Doctrine at St John's College, Nottingham (1979–85), and then led a church in Croydon until retiring in 1994.

The professor of theology was leaving the 18th green of the golf course when his partner for the round turned to him and, out of the blue, said, 'You know, Professor, what your church needs is revival.' 'Yes, indeed,' he answered, 'but the question is, what kind of revival?' The reply came, 'As far as I am concerned, *any kind of revival!*'

That conversation took place over 50 years ago, but if it was relevant then, the questions it raises are a hundred times more relevant in our own time, when the numerical decline of churches is being relentlessly recorded. Many Christians are more bewildered than committed, and tempted to conform to the ways of the society around them rather than witnessing to it and confronting it with

> **The numerical decline of churches** is being relentlessly recorded

> Often after decades of waiting, God acts dramatically to revitalize his people

...the God of resurrection who can work even in a spiritual cemetery

a way of life that has been radically transformed by the gospel of Christ.

In such circumstances, it is not surprising if many look back to similar periods of decline in the life of the Christian community to discover how, often after decades of waiting, God acts dramatically to revitalize his people. They remember what happened at the Protestant Reformation with leaders such as Luther and Calvin—and in the Catholic Counter-Reformation with leaders such as Loyola and the Jesuits. Then there were the great evangelical revivals in Britain and America under Wesley and Whitfield, resulting in the social reforms like the abolition of slavery celebrated this year.

Remembering all that and contemplating the state of the contemporary church and the contemporary world, many Christians are indeed saying that what we need is revival, and they are praying that what God did in the past for his people, he would do again for us and for our world today.

But the question 'What kind of revival?' does arise, and we would do well to pause and consider before we give the golfer's answer: 'any kind of revival'. People have hailed as revivals outbursts of religious fervour that have turned out to be merely emotional and ephemeral and have left participants more frustrated and disillusioned than ever. Furthermore, both Old and New Testaments give us passages set in quite different historical contexts but bearing a united witness to what is likely to happen when God revives the life of his people. What we are invited to seek and pray for is not 'any kind of revival' but the kind of revival that God has, in fact, promised.

We may think of Ezekiel 37, where God's people in exile in Babylon are realizing that nothing less than a revitalizing intervention by God can get them back into possession of the land and the heritage of which their sin has deprived them.

The present condition of the people is pictured as

a cemetery of dry bones, and when God asks the prophet if there is any possibility of life in such a situation, he can only reply, 'O Sovereign Lord, you alone know' (v. 3, NIV). When life has so far departed, only the giver of life himself will be able to restore it. There can be revival only when we turn away from all hope in what we can do for ourselves and start trusting in what God can do for us.

This story tells us that the giver of life will, in his grace, do for us what we could never do alone, but he will do it in his own way and in his own time. He will show himself to be the God of resurrection who can work even in a spiritual cemetery. He will awake to responsiveness those who have long been deaf to his voice, and he will make his word powerful and mighty to bring life to those to whom every possibility of life seems closed: 'Thus says the Lord God to these bones: Behold, I will cause breath to enter you, and you shall live… and you shall know that I am the Lord' (vv. 5–6, RSV).

This he will do at the time of his choosing, through the man of his choosing and by the means of his choosing. Israel's exile has been long; its needs have been carefully diagnosed; its renewal has been anticipated and prayed for but the years have passed and the situation has got worse rather than better. Delay has led to despair. Then, at last, God's moment comes, which his people can neither force nor predict, and the word goes out to Ezekiel: 'Prophesy to these bones' (v. 4). The things you had begun to think you would never see are going to happen now, right before your eyes. The days of death and exile are over and the days of life have come.

In the century before the Reformation, many attempts were made to reform a corrupt and failing church. All over Europe there were little groups of people praying for the life that only God could give, and dying before their prayers were answered. God's hands can never be forced, not even by the prayers of his people, but at the moment of his choosing the answer comes, as it did through Luther and later

Loyola and, in a similar situation some two centuries later, through Wesley and Whitfield.

When it does come, it is through the word and the Spirit. God's recipe for revival always has at its heart a radical and demanding re-engagement with the word of the gospel that will reorder the whole life of the church. When the church loses interest in the Bible, it cuts itself off from the source of its life. The first sign that revival is on the way is that the message of the Bible is taken so seriously that it can rearrange the personal and corporate lives of God's people. Real revival is far more than an outburst of religious emotion; when life comes, not only is the heart warmed but the mind is informed and reformed.

As Paul puts it to the Romans at the end of a passionate exposition of the gospel, 'Do not be conformed to this world, but be transformed *by the renewing of your minds*, so that you may discern what is the will of God—what is good and acceptable and perfect' (12:2, NRSV). The struggles and controversies that the churches are going through at the moment are part of the process that Paul is describing here. God's people are trying to discern what it means, in different areas of their lives, not to be conformed to the standards of the world but rather transformed according to the will of God. Struggles that engage mind, will and feeling can be seen as the essential reshaping of our lives which is the first stage of revival.

The way in which the gospel, in the power of the Spirit, restructures the people of God can be seen in Acts 2. There, what starts as an intense personal experience leads to the whole restructuring of the young Christian community's relationships in a new and unlimited commitment to God, to one another and to the witness of the church to the world: 'They devoted themselves to the apostles' teaching and to the fellowship, to the breaking of bread and to prayer... And the Lord added to their number daily those who were being saved' (2:42, 47, NIV).

The whole passage is a description of normative

> When the church loses interest in the Bible, **it cuts itself off from the source of its life**

> **God has his chosen times when he moves into top gear**

New Testament revival, which starts with personal experience and leads to new ways of thinking, new expressions of fellowship and new outreaches in mission. A revival is a genuine work of God in so far as it produces these results in the life of God's people. If any of these elements is lacking, the revival will be short-lived and fail in the purposes for which God gave it.

Of course, all these things happen all the time through the faithful ministries of word and sacrament, but in seasons of revival the breath of the Spirit turns into the rushing mighty wind of Pentecost. God has his chosen times when he moves into top gear, as Ezekiel also knew: 'Thus says the Lord God: "Come from the four winds, O breath, and breathe upon these slain, that they may live." I prophesied as he commanded me, and the breath came into them, and they lived, and stood on their feet, a vast multitude' (37:9–10, NRSV). In such times, the quiet work of the Spirit in the heart becomes public and dramatic and shows itself to be effective not just in the hidden depths of the believer but in the transformation of the Church's life, to make it effective in its impact on the world.

Such days are days of resurrection and we long to see them. Resurrection is always an act of God that is in his sovereign control. It is not something that any of our techniques can produce or control. Revival, like the Spirit at the heart of it, is always mysterious and God-given. We can pray for it but we cannot contrive it and, in God's good time and pleasure, that prayer will surely be answered.

In our longing for revival, we need also to remember that the God who reveals himself in the high days of Easter is also the God who is secretly but powerfully at work in the dreadful darkness of Calvary, where he seems to be absent. God is with us now in the days of the Church's defeat and decline, and is making us ready for the third day when the dead bones will live and the mighty winds of the Spirit will blow. ■

...nothing less than a revitalizing intervention by God can get them back into possession of the land

Struggles
that engage mind, will and feeling

Strangely warmed

Jean Watson, an ex-MK (missionary kid) brought up in China, trained as a teacher but took up writing when her three children were small and is now a grandmother to their three children. She is currently training to be a spiritual director.

> I have been looking back or looking around to identify my **past and present 'thin places'**

I began collecting my own 'remarkable things'

'I felt my heart strangely warmed.' John Wesley famously used these words in describing his conversion in 1738. Unlike him, I am not able to pinpoint a time and place for an initial conversion experience, but I have felt my heart 'strangely warmed', and not just once but many, many times.

Celtic Christians used different words to identify 'strangely warmed' or 'strangely awed' kinds of experiences. They spoke of these as 'thin places', by which they meant, I think, locations and situations in which the dividing line between the visible and invisible worlds —between God and his creation, between God transcendent and God immanent—seemed to disappear.

I came across the term only a few years ago but ever since then I have been looking back or looking around to identify my past and present 'thin places'. I first began to understand what the term meant through a talk I attended. The speaker waxed very eloquent about creation's beauty and wonder; it was in such contexts that he seemed to experience his 'thin places' most often.

More than I ever used to, I experience them there, too. Writing this article on a bright autumn day, I look out of the window and feel my spirits lifting at the sight of leafless trees etched against the sky by fingers of sunlight. The scene is a little herald to me of hope and its divine source. However, my 'thin places'— and perhaps this has something to do with gender as well as temperament—are more often experienced within social, relational contexts.

My primary boarding school was run by missionaries for missionaries' children and the regime was anything but soft. Then a new teacher arrived who was different, and one day she held my hands gently and looked long and thoughtfully at them before remarking with a smile, 'What capable little hands!' Suddenly, I was walking on air, feeling good about myself.

Much, much later in my life, I came to understand why this incident and many others like it stood out in my mind and affected me as they did, and I now try to be on the lookout for these types of encounters and experiences and to savour them as fully as possible.

> **God's subtle touches on our lives, touches of love, encouragement or challenge**

Some years ago, I read a book called *If Nobody Speaks of Remarkable Things* by Jon Macgregor (Bloomsbury, 2002) and was so struck by the contents and the title that I began collecting my own 'remarkable things'. They turned out to be very much in the 'thin places', 'strangely warmed or awed' category.

I made a note, for example, of a story I heard of a couple whose son had been swept away in the tsunami of Boxing Day 2005. Later, they revisited the scene of this terrible tragedy in order to set up a trust in their son's name to help other bereaved and injured survivors. I was very moved to see TV coverage of children painting pictures and speaking about their traumatic experiences, beginning the journey back to recovery and

Self-service tickets

Self-service tickets

7

8

© Doug Menuez/ Getty Images

healing, thanks to the incredible compassion, imagination and courage of those two people.

On a much smaller, more ordinary scale, I try to take note of people who 'do good in minute particulars'—such as 'freegans', those who collect and share food thrown out by hotels but perfectly edible, or 'guerrilla gardeners', who turn derelict or detritus-strewn areas into beautiful and peaceful parks and gardens, and many others like them about whom we hear so little in comparison with the coverage given to vandals, muggers and terrorists.

I also note down personal events that could be dismissed as totally trivial and mundane, such as one that took place at a railway station one day. I would have missed my train because of the long, slow-moving queue at the ticket office window had not a schoolboy showed me how to operate the ticket machine. He did this without the slightest trace of scorn or of a patronizing attitude towards someone whom he could so easily have written off as an elderly technophobe.

Why do such incidents and others like them mean so much to me and to others? I believe it is because we have come to see these experiences as God's subtle touches on our lives, touches of love, encouragement or challenge. This is what makes them so meaningful for us and what makes the places and people involved very special for us as well.

For me, it is the nudges of love and encouragement that mean the most; they warm my heart and sometimes bring tears to my eyes. After my husband's sudden death more than eleven years ago, I and my immediate family and some friends had to travel up to London for the inquest. I

...it is the nudges of love and encouragement that mean the most

remember sitting on the train in anguish but at the same time gripped by the insight—revelation, almost—that love, the genuine article, was the most important thing in the world, even while I was experiencing its correlation to pain.

The love of people for me and my family after my husband's death—friends, acquaintances, strangers—has strangely warmed my heart over and over again in the years since that time. When people still invite me, as a person in my own right rather than as part of a couple, to go to the cinema or have Sunday lunch with them, I am transported to a 'thin place' where the God who

something is being accomplished,

although I don't know what or when or for whom

God is here

and quietly at work throughout his creation

sometimes seems to be absent or merely watching from a distance is suddenly, subtly 'up close and personal'.

Of course, there is often pain involved in these types of experiences. I find it sad to see my elderly father in his nursing home, so physically frail and limited now, but my heart is strangely warmed by the people who still continue to visit and write to him, and by seeing him being thoughtfully and kindly cared for. When I am there with him, watering his plants, dealing with his post, taking him and his Zimmer frame slowly up the corridor and back, holding his hands and trying to communicate with him, I feel that we are not alone, that we are in a very

'thin place', and that something is being accomplished, although I don't know what or when or for whom.

Christmas 2005 was another 'thin place' for me because of the presence of my newest grandchild, a boy for whom his parents had waited and endured much anguish and many disappointments. The past pain made the present joy all the greater.

I was asked recently what I really wanted most in the world and, after some thought, I replied that I wanted those whom I loved to thrive and, if possible, to be part of that thriving myself. I think that, for me, every sign of genuine human thriving, of love and goodness not being overcome by their opposites, is like a burning bush. There, like Moses, I can take off my shoes and feel warmed and awed. These signs are like ladders from earth to heaven, as in Jacob's dream, where I can thrill to the knowledge that God is here and quietly at work throughout his creation, and that his angels and agencies can be anyone, anywhere—even here and now; even you and me. ■

Keepers of the flame

The spirituality of the Amish community

I first heard about the Amish in 1984 when I went to see *Witness*, starring Harrison Ford and Kelly McGillis as a Philadelphia detective and an Amish widow. I enjoyed the film and still get a tingly kind of feeling when I think of the barn-raising sequence. There was some controversy around the film, though, and one dour protestor, writing to the Governor of Pennsylvania, Richard L. Thornburgh, remarked, 'We Amish feel we are serving as a tool to lure tourists to Lancaster County.' Paramount Pictures caused offence by showing Harrison Ford—dressed in Amish clothes— felling a beefy bully with a less than non-violent right hook. I understood the reaction but I suppose my response was typical of many neutral

Philip Wood is a community worker based in Enfield. He has been linked to the Mennonite constituency in England since the early 1980s.

Telling the story of any Christian tradition is **a bit like doing family history** observers. *Witness* was captivating and served as a motivation to find out more about this reclusive community.

Who are the Amish?

Telling the story of any Christian tradition is a bit like doing family history. Trying to remember who was whose second cousin once removed, why Great-Uncle Robert ran off with the family silver and how the far-flung

> At the centre of the quilt is a motif representing fire, **a symbol of the heritage and values of the community**

relatives from Italy ended up moving from Milan to Manchester can be confusing. Amish history is peppered with divisions, slumps and revivals, but basically they are descendants of the early 16th-century radicals known as Anabaptists (literally 'rebaptizers', in the words of their opponents), known for their community-

mindedness and sacrificial pacifism.

The Anabaptist movement divided into different streams, including the fully communitarian Hutterites and the Mennonites, who originated in the Netherlands and were named after their most prominent early leader, Menno Simmons. Persistent persecution forced many Anabaptists to live in inaccessible mountainous areas or to choose migration as a means of preserving their conscience. The Amish community began as a dispute between Alsatian and Swiss Mennonites in the 1690s, originating as a reform movement led by Jacob Amman. Political upheavals and continuing persecution led Mennonites and Amish to settle in the New World. After an 83-day voyage, the *Charming Nancy*, the first ship carrying large numbers of Amish settlers, arrived in Philadelphia in 1737.

Keepers of the flame

Shipshewana is one of those small towns in Indiana that seem unremarkable. Inside the town hall, however, an unusual quilt is displayed—work influenced by both Native American and Amish traditions. The town website explains that this quilt is a 'visual prayer', which, in part, celebrates the Potawatomi tribe, known as the 'Keepers of the fire'. There is a prayer alongside the quilt, concluding with the words 'May we be vigilant "keepers of the fire", which are the values that form the heart of this community guiding those coming on the trail behind us!'

At the centre of the quilt is a motif representing fire, a symbol of the heritage and values of the community, which, like a fire, are kept lit for future generations, so that they may know the way home.

In many ways, this quilt is descriptive of the Amish as well as the Potawatomi. There is a fire burning at the heart of Amish corporate life, which is the spirit of community. In his fascinating and readable book, *The Riddle of Amish Culture*, Donald Kraybill explores the hidden wisdom beneath the apparent contradictions of the Amish attitude to technology. What are we to make of people who do not drive cars but have no qualms about employing their Mennonite neighbours to operate a taxi service? How do we understand the Amish practice of disallowing telephones in the home but allowing a 'phone shanty' to be shared between several households?

To be Amish is to walk or ride without hurry

All of that can seem like contradiction—like having your cake and eating it—but there is deep wisdom here. What seems like compromise actually arises from the love of community—a profound reflection on the unintended consequences of technology and a life-enhancing passion for every cherished detail of corporate life. In the case of the telephone, the Amish perception is that home-based telephones lead

Amish have a more profound insight into the nature of technology than many of us who accept the latest development without question.

> **A negotiation with modernity,** with the aim of preserving the vital spark of community

…a life-enhancing passion for every cherished detail of corporate life

to constant interruptions and separation in family and community as time is spent on individual conversation rather than family life. The issues are similar with regard to the car. Car ownership would increase mobility but would also bring with it social fragmentation as families opted to spend more time away from home.

The question the Amish ask in accepting this or that aspect of modernity is not, 'Is it too modern?' but rather, 'Does it nourish community?' Their attitude is far from obscurantist. It is a negotiation with modernity, with the aim of preserving the vital spark of community. When the cultural climate is hostile and the wind is blowing, what shall we do to keep the flame burning? Perhaps, in rejecting aspects of modern life, the

Slow church coming?

If there is one word that captures the heart of traditional Anabaptist spirituality, it is the German word *Gelassenheit*. The word is multi-textured but in this case it may be translated 'submission to God in community'. For Anabaptists, it came to articulate core beliefs and a way of life including simplicity, non-resistance, a rejection of individualism, organizations with a human scale and even humility in dress or mannerisms. Although *Gelassenheit* is under pressure among many of the descendants of the early Anabaptists, the Amish have preserved much of the original force of the word in their corporate life.

An interesting example is to be found in the Amish attitude to time. Kraybill cites an account of an Amish woman who had her garden professionally landscaped. The community disapproved, describing what she did as 'a little on the fast side'. To be 'fast' is to sail close to the wind of innovation—out of step with the rhythm of Amish life. To be Amish is to walk or ride without hurry. It is the slow life, timed to a pace that nurtures togetherness. While society moves ever faster by car and by plane, the Amish travel by buggy. As most Christians worship weekly, the Amish meet fortnightly, although the day is as unhurried as other aspects of Amish life. Worship lasts from around 7.30am to around 3.30pm and each slow, chant-like song may last for as long as 20 minutes.

The Amish are modern people and do not choose to reject every technological innovation, but slowing down the pace of progress serves to place new developments on probation—to subject change to corporate discernment. It would be easy to dismiss the Amish as a footnote to Christian history if it were not for the profound relevance of their life and spirituality to Christian discipleship in today's world.

The pain of our ecological crisis has thrown a spotlight on environmental damage as the sum of human thoughtlessness. Sadly, many Christians are not ready to respond to this crisis. All too often, members of mainstream churches have fewer problems with technological innovation than the Amish because we are not predisposed to think critically about intended or unintended consequences. Decisions (which, for the Amish, are matters of collective discernment) are devolved to the individual conscience. What passes as 'fellowship' in many congregations is inadequate for shaping a life that is distinctive from the wider culture.

Individual Christians, by and large, are not even aware that there is an issue with technology and, when they do develop awareness, it is as likely to come from the media as from church. 'Community', as it is experienced by most contemporary Christians, sometimes involves subscription to a set of shared convictions but frequently fails to make its way into everyday life: money, family, homemaking, work, possessions or travel.

A fire burning at the heart of Amish corporate life, **which is the spirit of community**

The average Amish family has 6.6 children, 80 per cent of whom remain within the Amish community. Demographics could be one reason why the Amish are unconcerned 'speed kills'. For many Christians searching for a way ahead, congregational life provides limited assistance. Some are wondering how well adapted the church of the future will be to model a form of corporate life which (to use the current jargon) leaves a positive 'footprint' on the earth. Is there a slow church coming? ■

about evangelism but, even if they were, how many people would be in the queue to join up? Becoming Amish is not an option for most of us, yet there are crucial lessons to be learned from these community-minded, steady-paced people. We live in a hurried world but, as road safety advice has it,

Something to read

Donald B. Kraybill, *The Riddle of Amish Culture*, Johns Hopkins University Press, 1989.

The Beloved

I saw him in the quiet
suburbs of my mind,
on the fringe of eternity
walking the halls of God.
A pure and living flame
touching with his presence
the blessed of his Father,
the light of the world
become the radiance of Heaven
and the new earth.
Where saints tread safely
surrounded by his abiding love.

EUNICE M. CARTER

Music for the soul:

O ye fire and heat, bless ye the Lord

Gordon Giles is vicar of St Mary Magdalene's Church, Enfield, north London. He contributes to BRF's 'New Daylight' notes and has also written 'The Music of Praise' (2002), 'The Harmony of Heaven' (2003) and 'O Come, Emmanuel' (2005) for BRF.

There is a frightening story from the book of Daniel about three men, Shadrach, Meshach, and Abednego, who are cast into a furnace because they will not worship a golden image set up by King Nebuchadnezzar of Babylon, in whose land they are in exile (Daniel 3:1–30). While the men who throw them into the fire are burnt to death, the three survive and are seen walking about with a fourth figure, whom Nebuchadnezzar describes as looking 'like a son of the gods' (v. 25, NIV). Amazed at their faith and endurance, he releases them and decrees that their faith, Judaism, should thereafter be respected.

In the Greek version of the Old Testament, the men's release is followed by a hymn of praise, which

> The particular reference to **'fire and heat'** is begun dramatically in the low voices

O all ye Works of the Lord, bless ye the Lord: praise him, and magnify him for ever. O ye Angels of the Lord, bless ye the Lord: praise him, and magnify him for ever. O ye Heavens, bless ye the Lord… O ye Sun and Moon, bless ye the Lord… O ye Stars of Heaven, bless ye the Lord… O ye Fire and Heat, bless ye the Lord… O ye Lightnings and Clouds, bless ye the Lord… O ye holy and humble Men of heart, bless ye the Lord… O Ananias, Azarias and Misael, bless ye the Lord: praise him, and magnify him for ever.

FROM 'THE SONG OF THE THREE' (THE BENEDICITE), DANIEL 3:57–88 (BCP VERSION)

MUSIC: HENRY PURCELL (1659–95)

…it has various musical settings

The full choir give a rich texture

in most Bibles is now separately listed in the Apocrypha section as 'The Song of the Three'. Originally, in the Latin Vulgate (and translations of it), it appears as Daniel 3:23–90, fitting in between verses 23 and 24. Despite this complexity, the thanksgiving uttered by the three after their deliverance has found its way into the Book of Common Prayer and is known as the Benedicite ('Bless ye the Lord'). Thus it has a fascinating origin and is a great hymn of praise, offering thanks to God for almost every aspect of creation we might think of, including, of course, 'fire and heat', two features that would have been literally close to the hearts of Shadrach, Meshach, and Abednego.

As a hymn of praise and thanksgiving, it has various musical settings, one of the most beautiful of which is by the great 17th-century English composer Henry Purcell, who devoted almost all of his relatively short life to the service of church music. He began as a chorister at the Chapel Royal; when his voice broke at the age of 14, he became a tuner of organs and wind instruments. In 1679 he became the organist of Westminster Abbey, and in

1682 he also became organist of the Chapel Royal, taking part in the coronations of James II and of William and Mary. His relationship with the ecclesiastical authorities had its ups and downs, but by the time of his untimely death he had earned himself a free funeral and a grave in Westminster Abbey, which can still be visited.

His setting of the Benedicite comes from a complete set of ten canticles that he wrote for use at Matins and Evensong. As such, these canticles (which include Magnificat, Nunc Dimittis and Jubilate) are still very much in use today; Purcell was paid 30 shillings for the complete set in September 1681. The text of the Benedicite is rather long and repetitive, but Purcell uses it complete, with all of the 'Praise Him, and magnify Him forever' refrains. Each verse ends with this praise clause, yet, in most places where the Book of Common Prayer is used today, it is only uttered on every third verse, shortening the canticle but also affecting the natural rhythms of the poetry. *Common Worship* has a complete modern English version, but also a briefer eight-verse version for those who need to abbreviate their praise of God, the creator of absolutely everything.

For this is what the Benedicite is: a comprehensive romp through every conceivable thing (to its authors) for which God might be praised. That's why we hear not only of sun and moon but of beasts and snow and fire and heat. All are entreated to join in praise of their Creator God: even the whales sing God's praise in their unique way! As we progress from the heavens, through the elements, the weather, the animal and plant kingdoms down to humanity, we notice a sweeping inclusiveness that ultimately concludes with the mysterious characters of Ananias, Azarias and Misael. Azarias (or Azariah) is actually Abednego, Misael is Mishak, and Annanias (Hananiah) is Shadrach; so what we have in the *Benedicite* is a direct reference to these survivors of the burning

Even the whales sing God's praise in their unique way

...everything in heaven and earth **harmoniously united in praise**

fiery furnace. The names in Daniel are the Babylonian ones given them by Nebuchadnezzar, whereas the other names are their Hebrew ones.

Purcell's nine-minute work sets this hymn of deliverance in a joyful way, beginning with a bass solo, arising from the deep, stating the purpose of the whole work: 'O all ye Works of the Lord, bless ye the Lord.' When we reach the phrase 'O ye sun and moon', the mood changes and becomes more serene as voices alternate across the space of the church, usually with a choir on either side creating a dialogue effect (antiphony). The full chorus sings, 'Praise him and magnify him forever', and the particular reference to 'fire and heat' is begun dramatically in the low voices followed by some polyphonic (multi-layered) writing. Other antiphonal verses—'O ye Nights and Days' and 'Light and Darkness'—follow. The choirs join forces again in lively manner for 'O let the earth' and then they calm down for a languid section, 'O ye mountains'.

Sometimes it sounds like chamber music; at other times the full choir give a rich texture, all providing contrast in a text that is both concise and comprehensive. At other times there is vocal illustration: for example, the lower voices are the 'fowls and beasts' while the boys' voices are the 'children of men'. Similarly, the men sing as the 'servants of the Lord' and the boys are the angelic 'spirits and souls' of the dead. Then, on a joyous note, Purcell concludes his depiction of everything in heaven and earth harmoniously united in praise of our loving, saving Creator God. ■

Readings for reflection

Daniel 3:1–30
The Song of the Three

Music to listen to

'Benedicite' by Henry Purcell, on *Anthems for the Chapel Royal* sung by Trinity College Cambridge Choir, directed by Richard Marlow (Conifer, ref: CLASS 7063).

Useles fires

'Blind Spots in the Bible' (BRF, 2006) presents bestselling author Adrian Plass's reflections on a range of Bible passages that are both intriguing and puzzling. They can raise hard questions and challenge us to think more deeply about what we believe and why—if we take time to read them properly.

'Now implore God to be gracious to us. With such offerings from your hands, will he accept you?'—says the Lord Almighty.

'Oh, that one of you would shut the temple doors, so that you would not light useless fires on my altar! I am not pleased with you,' says the Lord Almighty, 'and I will accept no offering from your hands. My name will be great among the nations, from where the sun rises to where it sets. In every place incense and pure offerings will be brought to me, because my name

My name will be great among the nations, from where the sun rises to where it sets

will be great among the nations,' says the Lord Almighty.

'But you profane it by saying, "The Lord's table is defiled,"and, "Its food is contemptible." And you say, "What a burden!" and you sniff at it contemptuously,' says the Lord Almighty.
MALACHI 1:9–13a (TNIV)

The music rose and fell and ebbed and flowed with flawless precision

'Useless fires.' The phrase jumped out at me. How many useless fires are lit in Christian churches around the world every Sunday, fires that crackle and pop and are filled with colour, but offer no genuine heat to the chilled body of Christ? This can happen for many reasons. I remember, for instance, speaking at a church on the borders of Scotland and England where the worship time preceding my talk was about as perfect in technical musical terms as it could be. The music rose and fell and ebbed and flowed with flawless precision, while the singers sang so skilfully and in such perfect harmony that it was a joy to listen. And yet...

What is the element missing from otherwise excellent church music when it just does not work? That was my feeling as I sat and listened to the instrumentalists and the vocalists. Something essential was absent from all those carefully organized sounds. Spiritual confidence, perhaps? A detachment from the roots of worship? A lack of heart? I found out later. Days earlier, the minister of the church had admitted to long-term adultery with a member of his congregation, and the technical near-perfection of the music was a desperate attempt to paper over deep cracks that had opened in the church community. That worship session never reached heaven and it never left the ground. Facts and feelings need to be faced. Tears and silence would have been more useful. It was a useless fire, and it warmed nobody.

A very similar point is made in the first chapter of Isaiah.

'The multitude of your sacrifices—what are they to me?' says the Lord. 'I have more than enough of burnt offerings, of rams and the fat of fattened animals; I have no pleasure in the blood of bulls and lambs and goats...

'I will not listen. Your hands are full of blood; wash and make yourselves clean. Take your evil deeds out of my sight! Stop doing wrong, learn to do right! Seek justice, encourage the oppressed. Defend the cause of the fatherless, plead the case of the widow.'
ISAIAH 1:11, 15b–17

'Look,' says God, 'I don't actually want any of that stuff. I really don't. It does nothing for me. What I want is for you to be just and kind and to look after the poor. I would like you to be obedient. My Son was obedient to the point of death and that's why I'm able to welcome you home. Don't waste what he did. I wouldn't give you two pence for religion, not even some of the wild, sizzling stuff that's taken the place of burning animals nowadays. Be loving to me and to each other. That's the scent I love—and have always loved.'

This is a voice that many Christians do not want to hear. It's too natural, too godly, too liable to insinuate itself into the cracks between our humanity and our faith, supergluing the two together, making us whole but robbing us of all the old securities.

Scary and sweet, isn't it? Clearly, God has never been interested in useless fire, flowery words, hollow worship or religious camouflage. He wants us to get on with the things that really matter. It might also be worth reflecting on this well-known verse from James: 'Religion that God our Father accepts as pure and faultless is this: to look after orphans and widows in their distress and to keep

oneself from being polluted by the world' (1:27).

When my wife and I travelled to Zambia in 2004, the significance of this verse became all too apparent. The purpose of our trip was to look at the work being done by World Vision, particularly in connection with the

That worship session never reached heaven

AIDS pandemic that is devastating the population in that part of the world. The idea was to write a book about our experiences that would highlight the enormous need for more resources, not just in Africa but in many other parts of the world as well.

We saw sights and people that came close to breaking our hearts. As one local worker told us, the fabric of Africa is being torn apart. Because of poverty and sickness, it is often the case that children are no longer being taken in and cared for by relatives. On the contrary, there are many instances of houses and property being taken away from orphans, who are then left to fend for themselves in a world where there are no hand-outs, unless you are fortunate enough to benefit from what is being done by the many aid agencies that are undertaking inspiring but inadequate work in that part of the world. Widows are dying of AIDS and wondering what will happen to their children when they have gone. We met

...authenticity and action in faith runs throughout the Bible

One thing is for sure: God is not fooled by useless fire.

There will be a reckoning

some of them. Young children are caring for their younger brothers and sisters because there is no one else left to do it. Like many countries that lie under the dark shadow of the AIDS crisis, Zambia is full of widows and orphans in distress. Food, health facilities, self-sustaining projects and education are priorities in these places, but there is not enough money.

Do I believe what James says about true religion? Yes, I do. Am I aware of the crisis in countries like Zambia?

Yes, I am. What will I do? I shall stop studying my spiritual navel and sponsor a child. It costs less than £20 each month. If we all did it, we could change the world.

The theme of authenticity and action in faith runs throughout the Bible, and yet it continues to be a sort of deliberate blind spot for so many of us who call ourselves followers of Jesus. One thing is for sure: God is not fooled by useless fire. There will be a reckoning. ■

PRAYER

Father, later in Isaiah 1 we read these words: "'Come now, let us reason together," says the Lord. "Though your sins are like scarlet, they shall be as white as snow."' This is your kind invitation to us, and we gladly accept the opportunity to think through the way we have been thinking and behaving, so that the fire of our worship and praise will not be useless. Forgive us for neglecting those who need justice and support. Show me what I can do to represent your practical love to the world. I pray that my eyes will be open to the needs of the world.

Earth's crammed with heaven,
and every common bush afire with God:
but only he who sees, takes off his shoes;
the rest sit round it, and pluck blackberries...
ELIZABETH BARRETT BROWNING, 'AURORA LEIGH' (1857)

✜

Creatures of a day, what is a man? What is he not? Mankind
is a dream of a shadow. But when a god-given brightness
comes, a radiant light rests on men, and a gentle life.
PINDAR, *PYTHIAN ODES* (FIFTH CENTURY BC)

✜

Fire. The God of Abraham, the God of Isaac, the God of Jacob.
Not of the philosophers and intellectuals... The God of Jesus Christ.
BLAISE PASCAL (1623–62), WRITING OF THE EXPERIENCE LEADING TO HIS CONVERSION

✜

The trouble is that no devastating or redeeming fires
have ever burnt in my life... My life began by flickering out.
IVAN GONCHAROV, *OBOLOMOV* (1859)

✜

Faith is not simply a patience that passively suffers until the
storm is past. Rather, it is a spirit that bears things—with
resignations, yes, but above all, with blazing, serene hope.
CORAZON AQUINO (b. 1933)

✜

Wood already touched by fire is not hard to set alight.
AFRICAN PROVERB

The Fire of God's Presence

Ann Persson has enjoyed leading Quiet Days over a period of many years, formerly at her home at Highmoor Hall, which she and her husband Paul used as a place of retreat and creativity. Ann is also a BRF trustee. This is a meditation, followed by practical exercises, that she has written on the fire of God's presence.

The purging fire

Imagine you're sitting by the fireside and watching, fascinated, as the flames dance in the grate, the wood spits and crackles and the soot on the chimneybreast glows and dies, forming ever-changing patterns. Turn the lights off and you have an even more magical experience. The room is both lit and warmed by the fire and shadows move across the walls and ceiling.

Fire is a potent image in the Bible and a symbol of God's presence, as Moses discovered in the desert. God spoke to him from a burning bush and later guided the Israelites by a pillar of fire (Exodus 3:2; 13:21).

In the letter to the Hebrews it is

written, 'Worship God acceptably with reverence and awe, for our "God is a consuming fire"' (Hebrews 12:28–29, NIV). This can feel scary but it is also his way of refining us and deepening our relationship with him.

An incident comes to my mind from when I took part in an art therapy weekend. The theme was water and, in between the sessions, we were encouraged to be creative with a variety of media. As I worked on my own project, I became aware of one woman who was totally absorbed in building a boat out of scraps of card, string and fabric. It was about two feet long, very elegant and eventually painted all over in black, so that it looked like a funeral boat such as you might see in India.

In due course, she shared with the group that her mother had died when she was only 20 and now, ten years later, her father had died just nine months before our weekend. She was still deeply grieving and not quite sure how to move on in her life. After completing her boat, she knew what she needed to do, and that was to burn it prayerfully, in effect to let go of her grief and turn to face the future.

I will never forget standing beside her with two others as, solemnly, she set fire to her beautiful craft. I talked with her the other day, 13 years after the event, and she still looks back to that time as a defining, healing, pivotal moment in her life.

God desires to purify us of anything that would impede our progress as his disciples, and sometimes he uses challenging life circumstances to bring to the surface the fears, addictions or prejudices that need to be released.

A PRAYER

O Comforter, draw near,
within my heart appear,
and kindle it, thy holy flame
bestowing.

O let it freely burn,
till earthly passions turn
to dust and ashes in its heat
consuming;
and let thy glorious light
shine ever on my sight,
and clothe me round, the while
my path illuming.

FROM 'COME DOWN, O LOVE DIVINE', BIANCO DA SIENA

Reflection

Take time to think of something in your life that you need to let go of. It may be a difficult relationship, an unfulfilled longing, resentment, some unforgiveness or a bereavement.

Action

Write down on a piece of paper whatever has come to mind, with all the emotions that are involved, and, in a safe place, when you feel ready, set light to it. As you watch the paper burn, give the issue to God and let him bring his healing and his release.

41

...a defining, healing, pivotal moment in her life

The inward fire of spiritual passion, power and love is his gift

The inner fire

When God poured out his Holy Spirit on the disciples, family and friends of Jesus at Pentecost, he accompanied his action with an outward sign of 'tongues of fire that... came to rest on each of them' (see Acts 2:3). When we dedicate our lives to God, he comes to live in us by his Holy Spirit. He lights a fire, as it were, within us. The inward fire of spiritual passion, power and love is his gift. I cannot produce it by myself, but my responsibility is to guard the flame.

This came home to me at the end of a three-day retreat. It had been a very inspirational time in which God had given me fresh insights and a real sense of his presence, which led to renewed commitment on my part. I was afraid that when I left, the experience might evaporate in the hurly-burly of daily life. In my final prayer time there, I had a picture of a lit candle with a guard around it and I wrote down these words in my journal: 'My mature responsibility is to guard the flame that God has lit within my heart, which the buffeting winds of life could so easily blow out.'

Sometimes we say that we feel 'burnt out'. Not surprisingly, this is often the experience of those in ministry who have to use many words and share many experiences but in whom the fire of God's Spirit is burning low. When the flame of a candle has become very small, it is usually because wax has built up around the sides and needs scraping back to give the wick more oxygen to burn brightly. When we are experiencing 'burn out' and circumstances seem to have snuffed out our sense of God's fire within us, we need to pay attention to what is happening. We need to take steps to cut back where possible; to give ourselves some 'time out' with God and room to breathe and recover.

A PRAYER

From all that dims Thy Calvary,
O Lamb of God, deliver me.
Give me the love that leads the way,
The faith that nothing can dismay,
The hope no disappointments tire,
The passion that will burn like fire;
Let me not sink to be a clod;
Make me Thy fuel, Flame of God.
AMY CARMICHAEL

Reflection

Take time to become aware of the fire of God that burns within you, whether brightly or just a flicker, which expresses itself in the desire for a deeper relationship with him, a commitment to his kingdom and an understanding of his word and his ways.

Action

Light a tealight or small candle. Ask God to show you ways in which you can guard and protect the flame of his Spirit in you. Taking time to spend some 'quiet spaces' with him is one way, but you will think of others. ■

Conservation

*A conker lay discarded
in the dew-drenched grass,
burnished, polished, glowing
a fallen ember
from the fires of God's continual creation,
this morning of the day before September.*

*How wonderful—
this thing of smooth bright beauty
should hold the essence of a mighty chestnut tree,
its roots and knotty bark,
its candles white or red,
splayed-finger leaves
and dominating shape,
and even more if I had eyes to see,
as Mother Julian saw, for all the world to tell,
all of creation in a hazel shell.*

*Dear Father God,
who, open-handed, lends
your own-created world for us to tend,
permit us not to mar,
your care to borrow
to leave a world enriched
for those who come tomorrow.*

FRANCIS BUXTON

Refined by fire: the story of

Beauty from Ashes

Jennifer Rees Larcombe has a fruitful and long-established prayer, healing, speaking and writing ministry, more recently focused on helping people adjust to pain, loss and trauma. Her most recent book, 'Journey into God's Heart' (Hodder & Stoughton, 2006), tells her life story.

The house was on fire! I could feel the scorching heat and hear the roar of the flames. I knew I was dreaming but could not wake myself. Suddenly the scene changed, as it often does in dreams. The fire was out and I was wandering around the charred ruins of my home, searching in vain among the ashes for precious possessions.

The atmosphere of that dream lived with me for days, perhaps because, at the time, my life felt like a burned-out home. I had recently been hit by a serious of catastrophic losses that had torn away most of what had previously been important to me, including the breakdown of my marriage.

Like most grieving people, I could not face long passages of scripture, but friends used to send me verses on cards or ring me with a scripture reference. I wrote them on scraps of paper and stuck them on my kitchen

He has sent me to
bind up the brokenhearted
... to comfort all who mourn
.... to bestow on them
crown of beauty
... of ashes

Isaiah 61. 1-3

...to bestow on them a crown of beauty instead of ashes

wall, but it was the one over the kettle that spoke to me louder than any other: 'He has sent me to bind up the broken-hearted... to comfort all who mourn... to bestow on them a crown of beauty instead of ashes' (Isaiah 61:1–3, NIV).

These words, though written 700 years before his birth, described the mission of Jesus: we see him doing exactly these things throughout the Gospels—and he has carried on ever since. When your life is suddenly destroyed, you just can't believe that you will ever be happy again, but the one who said, 'I have come that they may have life, and have it to the full' (John 10:10) never intended us to live a half-life, hiding among the ashes of our dreams and hopes. There really is hope for broken lives.

Perhaps, for me, the turning point came when I discovered a little prayer written by Leanne Payne: 'Lord, transform this anguish into healing grace for others.' Hope was relit when I stopped seeing all that I was going through as a useless waste and began to wonder if, one day, God might even use it.

At first it seemed likely that I would lose my home, which felt like one of the biggest griefs of all. My husband and I had bought it for a very definite purpose, soon after an amazing thing had happened to us. I had been ill and confined to a wheelchair for eight years, but quite suddenly the Lord had healed me through the prayers of a new Christian. The experience of all those years of illness had shown us God's deep compassion for people whose lives had been smashed, but the healing made us appreciate his power to intervene and bring restoration.

My husband had been working as a schools inspector but we both longed to be in full-time Christian ministry, so we had begun asking the Lord what direction he wanted us to take. At the time, we were living in a terraced house in the middle of a busy town but one day, during a prayer meeting with friends, I saw a very clear picture in my head. I was standing in a beautiful garden, deep in the country, surrounded by woods and fields. I saw a courtyard with a fountain and beyond was a little room. The door stood open and, even though I did not go in, I knew that God himself was there. A long line of people were trudging through the courtyard and, one by one, they went through the door.

'Why are they here, Lord?' I whispered.

'They've all been broken physically, emotionally or spiritually and need my healing touch.' The words were as clear as if my ears had heard them, and somehow I knew that God wanted us to help him turn that picture into reality, so we sold our town house and scoured the countryside for the right property. When the agents sent us details of a little three-bedroom bungalow surrounded by a jungle, it certainly did not look promising on paper, but the moment we arrived on the doorstep we *knew* it was the place God had chosen. We took a leap of faith and bought it! Soon we had restored the garden, created the courtyard with its fountain and, beyond it, we built the little prayer room. The 'wounded people' were just beginning to arrive when that vision was burned to ashes.

It felt so strange that God should give a vision like that and then allow it to be destroyed, yet humanly speaking there was no way I could continue with it without my husband. But we were not 'humanly speaking', and a group of friends offered me financial backing and their prayerful support and we launched the charity Beauty from Ashes.

> **I saw a courtyard with a fountain and beyond was a little room**

Its aim is to support those who are facing loss, grief and trauma of all kinds. By that time, I had trained as a counsellor and teamed up with a retired GP called Jenny Brown and a number of others, all skilled in counselling and prayer ministry but who had also survived major losses. Our work with people has grown out of our own pain but we also know that the promises in Isaiah 61 still apply. Jesus can, and does, mend broken hearts.

The line of people who come for help every day is now so long that we use not only the prayer room but also the bedrooms, the summer house and a caravan.

An organization like Beauty from Ashes would never have been necessary in the past, when families and communities stayed close, when people had time to listen and grieving was an acceptable part of

It always saddens me to realize just how many of us carry secret loads of guilt or grief

In these high-speed, pressured days, grieving is unfashionable

life. In these high-speed, pressured days, grieving is unfashionable: we are urged to take a pill and move on with our lives as quickly as possible. Christians find the whole grief package, with its disconcerting bouts of anger, doubt, fears and depression, particularly hard to handle. We think, 'Christians shouldn't feel like this, we should be full of faith and joy.' But Christians are still human: they bleed if you cut them and grieve if they lose people they love.

Adjusting to sudden change always takes much longer than we expect, and those awkward emotions that accompany loss need to be talked out and listened to by someone who understands. Like Job in the Bible, many of our visitors feel their faith in a loving God is wobbling badly. 'Why has he allowed all this to happen to me?' is a question they often ask. Their Christian friends often seem very like Job's tactless 'comforters', heaping them with condemnation, unhelpful advice or tactless clichés. The 'Jobs' who come to us often find the most comfort from talking to someone who has experienced, but also survived, a similar loss.

A high percentage of those coming to Beauty from Ashes are church leaders or in prominent positions in Christian work. They often feel as if they are 'grieving in a goldfish bowl'. 'I know I need help,' said J on her first visit, 'but where does a vicar's wife go when her husband leaves her for a member of his congregation? All my friends at church are too traumatized to come near me and I'm an embarrassment to the bishop. Yet I've lost my home, my church, my role in the community, as well as my husband, my vicar and my financial security.' J came to us regularly over the next three years, and watching the way the Lord slowly and gently rebuilt her blessed us all. Sadly, many are in her situation, now that Christian marriages are breaking up with such hideous regularity.

We also run regular Quiet Days here. Just sitting still in a garden and listening to God can be very healing.

'I came to one of your Quiet Days a few years ago,' wrote P recently. 'At the time I was seriously considering leaving my husband, our busy manse and teenage sons. I wanted to start a new life with someone I had met at work, but the Lord spoke to me that day, most decisively. I returned to Beauty from Ashes several times after that, to pray with one of your team. Together we worked through the underlying cause of my desire to run away and I'm glad to say that, with God's help, the crisis is over.'

It always saddens me to realize just how many of us carry secret loads of guilt or grief, sometimes for many years. G came to us because she was chronically depressed: 'I hide it, particularly at work, but everything always feels grey and there's no joy left in life at all.' As she talked to two of us in the prayer room, she managed to put into words something she had never told anyone before: 'Sixteen years ago I had an abortion. We weren't married then, we were both working hard at university and a baby wasn't convenient. Now that we want a baby, I can't seem to conceive. I know God has forgiven me,' she finished sadly, 'but I can't forgive myself.'

G visited us regularly for some weeks and during that time she placed her lost baby in God's hands. We even buried a small, symbolic stone under the cross at the bottom of the garden. Unforgiveness so often impedes joy, but it is just as vital to forgive ourselves as it is to forgive someone else. One cold morning G told me, 'It may be winter out there in the garden, but inside my heart I can feel the spring coming. Life

'I know God has forgiven me,' she finished sadly, 'but I can't forgive myself.'

suddenly has colour again.' Later that year, she rang to tell me she was pregnant and I now have her baby's photo stuck on my kitchen wall.

We know that it is not our counselling skills that help people; it is connecting them with the living Christ himself through prayer and his word. The scripture we often give our visitors to take home is from Isaiah 43:2–3: 'When you walk through the fire, you will not be burned; the flames will not set you ablaze. For I am the Lord, your God… your Saviour.' ∎

For more information, visit www.beautyfromashes.co.uk or write to: Beauty from Ashes, Hildenborough, Ashes Lane, Hadlow, Tonbridge, Kent TN11 9QU (tel. 01732 851146).

William Tyndale:

Let there be light

Caroline Hodgson is a writer and editor specializing in Christian material. She has written sermons, reflections and portraits of well-known Christians, including saints and missionaries. She lives in Hebden Bridge, West Yorkshire.

Reformers from John Wycliffe's day (1329–84) onwards have insisted that the Bible is the supreme source of Christian truth, that scripture needs no interpreter, and that God's word should be made accessible for all. Wycliffe oversaw the Bible translation that bears his name—but fire is a recurrent theme here, and Wycliffe's Bibles were burnt, as were his disinterred bones. Two hundred years later, the controversy still would not go away, and Henry VIII came to the throne in 1509, vowing to Pope Julius II that he would stamp out this persistent heresy. He had not counted on William Tyndale's influence.

Tyndale was born in Gloucestershire around 1494. He was educated at Oxford and Cambridge (possibly studying under Erasmus), where he met reformers Thomas Bilney and John Frith and became a strong supporter of the Church reform movement. The reformers believed that the Church had become corrupt, and that those in religious orders wielded power over the people through claiming special communication with God. They wanted to see the Bible made available even, as Tyndale put it, to 'a boy that driveth the plough'.

Around 1520, Tyndale became chaplain in the house of Sir John Walsh in Gloucestershire. His outspoken views involved him in controversy and he always resorted to the Bible as the supreme truth. As Foxe's *Book of Martyrs* puts it, he 'spared not to show unto them simply and plainly his judgment, and when they at any time did vary… in opinions, he would show them in the Book, and lay plainly before them the open and manifest places of the Scriptures, to confute their errors, and confirm his sayings'.

The disputes escalated until Tyndale was summoned before the Chancellor of the Diocese of Worcester on a charge of heresy. He became determined to translate the Bible into English himself and travelled to London to seek financial backing. But he was firmly rebuffed by Bishop Cuthbert Tunstall, who, like many highly placed churchmen, was uncomfortable with the idea of the Bible in the vernacular and realized that such a project would be politically explosive.

The only way Tyndale could pursue his vision was to leave England. He landed at Hamburg in 1524, having already begun to translate the New Testament. While in Germany, he visited Martin Luther at Wittenberg and waged a pamphlet war with the resolutely Roman Catholic Thomas More, who referred to Tyndale as a 'drowsy drudge' who had 'drunken… deep in the devil's dregs'.

Copies of Tyndale's New Testament arrived in England in 1526, to a hostile reception from the Church. Although numerous partial and complete translations had been made, Tyndale's was the first to take advantage of the new medium of print, which allowed for its wide distribution and made it

> …such a project would be **politically explosive**

harder than ever to suppress. Bishop Tunstall bought a huge quantity of the first edition and ordered them to be publicly burnt outside St Paul's Cathedral. This gave Tyndale the oxygen of publicity, cleared his debts and provided funds to carry on with his work.

Cardinal Wolsey condemned Tyndale as a heretic and demanded his arrest. Tyndale went into hiding and began work on the Old Testament and other treatises. By now almost revelling in his notoriety, he continued to rock the boat. In 1530, he wrote *The Practyse of Prelates*, in which he opposed Henry VIII's divorce and referred to Wolsey as 'Wolfsee… shipwrecke of all England'. He had alienated the king and most of the leaders of the established Church.

Henry VIII asked the Holy Roman Emperor Charles V to have Tyndale seized and returned to England. In 1535, he was betrayed to the authorities, arrested in Antwerp and held near Brussels. He was tried on a charge of heresy and condemned to the stake, despite the statesman Thomas Cromwell's attempted intervention on his behalf. On 6 October 1536, Tyndale was strangled and his dead body burnt. His final words were reportedly, 'Oh Lord, open the King of England's eyes.'

'Oh Lord, open the King of England's eyes'

Tyndale's was the first to take advantage of the new medium of print

Scholars still disagree about the original sources that Tyndale used, and the merits of his translation. It has to be said that his version is, in places, slanted towards his own inclinations. He translates 'bishop' into 'overseer', while 'priest' becomes 'elder'; for 'heresy' read 'choice', for 'martyr', 'witness', while 'evangelist' is translated as 'bearer of good news'.

But Tyndale's influence on the English language is indisputable: much of his work found its way to the King James Bible, published in 1611, and many of his phrases have passed into proverbial use. They include 'salt of the earth', 'let there be light', 'signs of the times', 'a law unto themselves', and 'fight the good fight'.

Tyndale fell into the faultline between the old order and the new. In July 1536, a few months before he died, the government issued the Ten Articles, the first formal statement of belief of the Church of England. At the same time, an injunction decreed that an English translation of the Bible—which drew heavily on Tyndale's work—was to be placed in every parish church. The Reformation would take a good many twists and turns after that, but it would surely have pleased Tyndale to see the word of God made so widely available.

Of course, Tyndale's original words now themselves represent the archaic form of the Bible, but, as such, they have a wonderful poetry, as this passage from 1 Corinthians 13 shows:

When I was a chylde I spake as a chylde I vnderstode as a childe I ymagened as a chylde. But assone as I was a man I put awaye childesshnes. Now we se in a glasse even in a darke speakynge: but then shall we se face to face. Now I knowe vnparfectly: but then shall I knowe even as I am knowen. Now abideth fayth hope and love even these thre: but the chefe of these is love. ■

The flame still burns in Whitby

And there appeared to them tongues like flames of fire, dispersed among them and resting on each one. And they were all filled with the Holy Spirit (ACTS 2:3–4, NEB).

It is said that in every Celtic monastery, a fire was kept burning continuously as a sign of God's presence with the inhabitants.

Hilda arrived in Whitby in 657. In those days, it was called Steonaeshalch, the Bay of Light. After she established her double monastery (accommodating both men and women) of wattle and daub huts, the glow of the fires must have lit up the whole area. Almost certainly, the monastery maintained a lighthouse that provided a guide to sailors travelling along the dangerous coast.

In the same way, Hilda's monastery became a place of guidance, of refuge, learning and community. She was renowned for her life of

Sister Dorothy Stella is Prioress (leader) of an Anglican religious community, the Order of the Holy Paraclete based in Whitby, North Yorkshire.

holiness, her wisdom and common sense. Bishops and priests came to the monastery for training; young women of noble birth were entrusted to her care. Everybody was welcomed, as Hilda was not only concerned with the politics of the church (she advised even bishops) but she also showed concern for all who lived around her monastery.

She encouraged the genius of Caedmon, a cowherd who had been given the gift of singing praise to God, and ensured that his verse was written down so that it became instrumental in laying the foundations for English indigenous poetry: 'Now must we praise the Guardian of heaven, the might of the Lord and his intentions, the work of the Father of Glory; for he, Eternal Lord, ordered each wonder' ('Song of Caedmon').

The flame of zeal for God's word burned in the hearts of all who lived in Hilda's monastery and spread far and wide. In 664, what became known as the Synod of Whitby was held there. Would the church follow the Roman way or the Celtic way? The future of the church in England was decided that day in the presence of Hilda.

After Hilda's death in 680, the religious life in Whitby continued until 869, when very different fires were lit—the flames of destruction kindled by the Vikings when they attacked and destroyed the monastery. Nevertheless, the sacredness of the place was never lost: in 1078, the Benedictine monk Reinfrid refounded the abbey on the site of Hilda's monastery and dedicated it to St Peter and St Hilda. This Benedictine abbey prospered until it was dissolved by Henry VIII in 1539.

It is the ruins of this abbey that dominate the skyline of Whitby today, a place to

A place of guidance, of refuge, learning and community

which thousands come in pilgrimage. It stands on the eastern cliff top, battered by wind and storm, in that wild place where Hilda chose to light her flame of Christianity. And while the flame of that monastery may have been extinguished twice, it was rekindled on the west cliff many years later.

A young woman, Margaret Cope, came to establish a monastery at Sneaton Castle on the west side of Whitby in 1915. She had been a novice in another community in West Yorkshire and, when the sisters there made the decision to close their school, novice Margaret was sure that God was calling her to found St Hilda's School and a new religious community dedicated to the Holy Paraclete (or Holy Spirit: 'Paraclete' is from the Greek *paracletos*, which means the Comforter, the Spirit). Like Hilda, she was a woman of vision and courage, also prepared to live on the edge. She moved into the castle at a time when the east coast of England was being bombarded by German planes.

Mother Margaret (as she became) wrote a rule for the Order, which is unique but influenced by both the Celtic and Benedictine monastic life. The centre of both was a life of prayer and both had a great sense of hospitality. Strangers were never turned away.

By 1921, Mother Margaret's community was growing and she had accepted an invitation to found a school in Cape Coast, Ghana. Opportunities followed for sisters to work in Zimbabwe, South Africa and Swaziland. This led to the founding of schools, colleges, a midwifery training college and hospital, babies' homes, vocational training schools, retreat and pastoral centres and, most recently, an eye clinic. Sisters still work in Ghana, South Africa and Swaziland. They have also worked in Sweden and, nearer home, in Northern Ireland and Scotland.

Like St Hilda's nuns, OHP sisters have faced danger. There was the risk, in war time, of being torpedoed at sea; the possibility, in Africa, of dying from sleeping sickness or malaria or from accident on the hazardous roads on which they often

The future of the church in England was decided that day in the presence of Hilda

The flame of zeal for God's word burned in the hearts of all

The monastery maintained a lighthouse that provided a guide to sailors

travelled. Sisters have lived through military coups, in places where there is little electricity, water or telephone communication and, at times, with little food. Over the years, thousands of girls have been educated and people helped and cared for through times of need and sickness.

At the centre of community life is faith and trust in a God who is around us and within us, guiding us, through the example of Jesus Christ whose way we follow and by the power of the Spirit who breathes life into us and is our protector.

The basis of each day is coming together four times to recite or sing the monastic Office, the set prayers for the season. This underpins and gives strength for the varied tasks of each day. As our Rule of Life explains, 'The Office is both an offering of praise to God and an act of intercession for the world. By it, the natural divisions of the day are hallowed and dedicated to him.'

We also live out the vows we make of poverty, celibacy and obedience. They express our total commitment to God and, by binding us to Christ, they free us to serve him in the church and the world. One of our greatest challenges is the living of the common life. To cite our Rule again, 'Each member is encouraged to make her own contribution to the whole and the needs of each are met with courtesy. The ideal of the Order is a balanced life of prayer, work and recreation in which every activity is regarded as sacramental.'

The centre of the Order is the priory at Whitby, where sisters begin and usually end their time in community. From here they have, and still do, set off on journeys, at times into the unknown, to work in jobs that are both exciting and challenging.

The work of St Hilda's School ceased in 1997, but the buildings have been transformed into a retreat and conference centre, used by parishes, schools and universities. Individuals and many small groups come to walk, to make music, to find peace and a quiet place. Many guests also find their way to the priory in search of a place of peace and refreshment. Tertiary and Associate members gain strength and inspiration from their connection with the community.

As the sisters of the Order of the Holy Paraclete continue to live their religious life in the footsteps of St Hilda, we remember how, in a time of violence, she created a place of peace. In a time when few were rich and many poor, she treated all with equal respect. In a time when many did not know Christ, she trained people to communicate the good news.

Hilda's final message to her community was, 'Maintain the Gospel of peace'. Other wise sayings attributed to her are:

- Trade with the gifts God has given you.
- Bend your minds to holy learning, that you may escape the fretting moth of littleness of mind that would wear out your souls. Brace your wills to action, that they may not be the spoils of weak desires.
- Train your hearts and lips to song, which gives courage to the soul.
- Being buffeted by trials, learn to laugh. Being reproved, give thanks. Having failed, determine to succeed.

These are not instructions for the faint-hearted, but women living the religious life in the Order of the Holy Paraclete try to live by them as they follow God's calling to lead the religious life within the Anglican Church in this century.

The flame still burns. ■

A balanced life of prayer, work and recreation in which every activity is regarded as sacramental

For more information about conference facilities and retreats at Sneaton Castle, visit the website www.sneatoncastle.co.uk (tel 01847 600051). You can also contact St Oswald's Pastoral Centre (tel: 01947 810496) and St Hilda's Priory (www.ohpwhitby.org; tel: 01947 602079).

Fire

These prayers are written by Amy Boucher Pye, an American who has lived in the UK for the past nine years. She works in Christian publishing and has written for such periodicals as 'Church Times', 'The Church of England Newspaper', 'Woman Alive' and 'Christian Marketplace'. She makes her home in north London with her husband and young family.

Fire in the Bible has different connotations: it can bring not only heat and comfort but also destruction and fear. The Lord God appeared as a guide to Abram and Moses in a smoking pot and burning bush, but he is also called a consuming fire. Our prayers focus on the varied image of fire as inspired by biblical text, and I hope that they will bring warmth, purification and comfort.

Sunday

There the angel of the Lord appeared to [Moses] in flames of fire from within a bush… 'Do not come any closer,' God said. 'Take off your sandals, for the place where you are standing is holy ground' (Exodus 3:2, 5, TNIV).

Lord God, you appeared to Moses as a burning bush—flames that burned but did not reduce to ashes. You provided him with warmth and light as you revealed yourself as the God of his ancestors, who had come to deliver his people from the misery of Egypt. Because you were there, Moses was standing on holy ground.

We are often like Moses, thinking that we are insufficient for the tasks to which you call us. But you are gracious, and promise to give us the words to speak. Help us to trust you and to follow your calling for our lives, that we might be your flames of light and cheer in a cold and unfeeling world.

Monday

When you walk through the fire, you will not be burned; the flames will not set you ablaze (Isaiah 43:2b).

Lord, you have promised to be with us through the fiery trials that we face in this life. Help us to cling to these promises when we feel overwhelmed or downtrodden.

Help us to remember the three friends of Daniel who were thrown into the fiery furnace but were unscorched because you were their shield around them.

Lord God, please burn a holy ring of fire around our homes and our loved ones, that we would remain unscathed by the things that would harm us. Thank you for your everlasting love and protection.

Tuesday

Consider what a great forest is set on fire by a small spark. The tongue also is a fire, a world of evil among the parts of the body (James 3:5–6a).

Lord Jesus, we confess that our tongue can be like a small flame that sparks

out of control. Forgive us for our gossip or unclean words: the unkind things we say to and about others; the words we let loose when we are angry or hurt.

Help us to have no unwholesome talk coming out of our mouths, but only that which is helpful for building up others. Give us a word of encouragement for another person today.

Inhabit our words when we praise you, that we would bring glory and honour to your name.

Wednesday

Suddenly a sound like the blowing of a violent wind came from heaven… They saw what seemed to be tongues of fire that separated and came to rest on each of them. All of them were filled with the Holy Spirit (Acts 2:2–4a).

Holy Trinity, through the Holy Spirit you appeared as a flame to the new Church. The tongues of fire rested on the believers and they were filled with your Spirit.

Come anew into our lives, that we would burst forth with praise and thanksgiving to your holy name. Thank you that when we invite you in, you inhabit our very souls and bodies, and we are never separate from you.

Give us the tongues of poets and the angels, that our speech may be delightful not only to our fellow humans but also to you. We come ready to be filled with your renewing Spirit.

Thursday

Dear friends, do not be surprised at the fiery ordeal that has come on you to test you… But rejoice inasmuch as you participate in the sufferings of Christ (1 Peter 4:12–13a).

Heavenly Father, we don't welcome the fiery trials we endure in this life. Strengthen us, that we might be given the wisdom and perseverance to endure to the end. Help us to look to you for release and freedom or, if our troubles continue, give us the fortitude to keep trusting in you.

We know, Lord, that while we are on this side of heaven our lives will not be free from sorrow. Impart to us your heavenly vision, that we may live in the light of eternity and anticipate that holy city where there will be no more tears, death, mourning or pain.

Reveal your glory in us, Lord Christ, as we participate in your sufferings. Refine us through your holy fire.

Friday

Another angel, who had a golden censer, came and stood at the altar… The smoke of the incense, together with the prayers of God's people, went up before God from the angel's hand (Revelation 8:3–4).

Father God, our prayers are offered as incense before you. Spark us out of our complacency when we are weary and do not want to pray. Give us the desire to seek your wisdom and direction in all that we do.

Help us, too, to worship you with clean hearts and hands. We ask that you would forgive us our sins—those things we do wilfully and the things we leave undone.

We also ask that you would help us to pray for others throughout the day. Love the world through us, and enlarge our vision for your work in and through us. May our prayers rise as incense before you.

Saturday

Then the Lord will create over all of Mount Zion and over those who assemble there a cloud of smoke by day and a glow of flaming fire by night; over everything the glory will be a canopy. It will be a shelter and shade from the heat of the day, and a refuge and hiding-place from the storm and rain (Isaiah 4:5–6).

Creator and Redeemer, you have given us this vision of the new heaven and new earth.

We pray that now, as then, you would be our shelter in the heat of the day, whether this is persecution, gossip or hardship. We pray that you will be our hiding place when we face the storms of life.

Come and dwell with us and wipe the tears from our eyes. Make all things new, we pray, for you are the Alpha and the Omega, the beginning and end. Come, Lord Jesus. ■

Late one night, at the age of 31, 17th-century French philosopher Blaise Pascal had an overwhelming experience of God, lasting two hours. He wrote a record of it on parchment and sewed it into his coat so it would go with him everywhere. Here is how his record begins.

The year of grace 1654. Monday, 23 November, feast of Saint Clement, Pope and Martyr, and of others in the Martyrology. Eve of Saint Chrysogonus, Martyr and others. From about half past ten in the evening until half past midnight. Fire.

Musings of a middle-aged mystic

Veronica Zundel is a journalist, author and contributor to 'New Daylight'. She has also written 'The Time of Our Lives' for BRF. She lives in north London.

I'm struck by the contrast between his precise note of the day, time and position in the church's year and then that single word: 'Fire'. It's as though language is totally inadequate to encompass what he has encountered—in fact, the fewer words, the better. In French, that single word would be even shorter: '*Feu*'.

Throughout the Bible, fire is an image used to describe the indescribable, the presence of God. Moses encounters God in the mystery of a bush that is on fire but doesn't burn away. The Israelites are guided through the desert by a pillar of cloud by day and a pillar of fire by night.

Throughout the Bible, fire is an image used to describe the indescribable, **the presence of God.**

What does this image of fire tell us about God?

Fire falls on Elijah's offering on Mount Carmel. Repeatedly, God is called a 'devouring' or 'consuming' fire (Deuteronomy 4:24; Psalm 50:3; Hebrews 12:29) of whom we should be in awe.

In a gentler mode, the travellers to Emmaus exclaim, 'Were not our hearts burning within us while he was talking to us on the road?' (Luke 24:32, NRSV). Many Christians, including a friend of mine, have felt an actual physical warmth around the heart as they prayed.

What does this image of fire tell us about God? Certainly that God is not to be messed with: every child is taught not to put their fingers in the fire. It is also an image of purification, in the context of smelting ore: 1 Corinthians 3:13 tells us that 'the fire will test what sort of work each has done'. 'When he has tested me,' declares Job confidently, 'I shall come out like gold' (Job 23:10).

Fire, from prehistoric times, has also been humanity's friend, though a friend that has to be treated with care. Fire gives light at night, keeps us warm, enables us to cook our food and keeps wild beasts away. Forest fires cleanse and nourish the forest, burning out weaker growth and fertilizing the new shoots with its ash—a kind of resurrection by fire.

We talk of being 'fired up' by an idea or 'carrying a torch' (a burning one!) for someone to whom we are attracted. Fire can signify what drives us to be creative, to follow our vision and achieve our goals. Tongues of flame burned over the apostles as they were filled with the Holy Spirit at Pentecost (Acts 2:3).

What difference would it make to our lives, our churches or our work if we were truly 'on fire' with the fire of God's calling? Not blazing with anger, or burning with judgmentalism, but like a flaming torch, a lamp set on a lampstand, lighting the way for others to see where God's goodness is to be found. Like fire itself, the idea is somewhat scary—but enticing, too. May we invite others to gather around God's hearth and know the warmth and security of God's presence. May we have a 'fire in the belly' for God's kingdom, for the peace and justice for which the earth, and its God, long. ■

Do take a moment to visit the Quiet Spaces website (www.quietspaces.org.uk) and email us with your thoughts, perhaps sparked by what you have read in this issue.

In our next issue

In 2007 *Quiet Spaces* has pondered rock, water and fire, three elemental aspects of nature. Next year we turn to a trio that every one of us experiences every single day of our lives: morning, noon and night. We begin (appropriately) with morning, a theme that has overtones of new life, of renewal and hope—yet, for those in difficult circumstances, the beginning of a new day can mean having to ready themselves for a fresh challenge.

Contact us at:

Quiet Spaces,
BRF,
15 The Chambers,
Vineyard, Abingdon
OX14 3FE
enquiries@brf.org.uk

Quiet Spaces is published three times a year, in March, July and November. To take out a subscription, please complete this form, indicating the month in which you would like your subscription to begin.

☐ I would like to give a gift subscription (please complete both name and address sections below)

☐ I would like to take out a subscription myself (complete name and address details only once)

This completed coupon should be sent with appropriate payment to BRF. Alternatively, please write to us quoting your name, address, the subscription you would like for either yourself or a friend (with their name and address), the start date and credit card number, expiry date and signature if paying by credit card.

Gift subscription name _____

Gift subscription address _____

_____ Postcode _____

Please send beginning with the next July / November / March issue: *(delete as applicable)*

(please tick box)	UK	SURFACE	AIR MAIL
Quiet Spaces	☐ £16.95	☐ £18.45	☐ £20.85

Please complete the payment details below and send your coupon, with appropriate payment to: BRF, 15 The Chambers, Vineyard, Abingdon OX14 3FE.

Name _____

Address _____

Postcode _____ Telephone Number _____

Email _____

☐ Please do not email me any information about BRF publications

Method of payment: ☐ Cheque ☐ Mastercard ☐ Visa ☐ Maestro ☐ Postal Order

Card no. ☐☐☐☐ ☐☐☐☐ ☐☐☐☐ ☐☐☐☐ ☐☐☐☐

Valid from ☐☐☐☐ Expires ☐☐☐☐ Issue no. of Maestro card ☐☐☐

Security Code ☐☐☐

Signature _____ Date ___ / ___ / ___

All orders must be accompanied by the appropriate payment.
Please make cheques payable to BRF
☐ Please do not send me further information about BRF publications

PROMO REF: QSFIRE
BRF is a Registered Charity